Harvest

by
Lois Markham

BLACKBIRCH PRESS, INC.

WOODBRIDGE, CONNECTICUT

Published by Blackbirch Press, Inc.
260 Amity Road
Woodbridge, CT 06525

©1999 by Blackbirch Press, Inc.
First Edition

e-mail: staff@blackbirch.com
Web site: www.blackbirch.com

Printed in the United States

10 9 8 7 6 5 4 3 2 1

Photo Credits
Cover: ©Patrick Ramsey/International Stock; page 3:
©Bob Firth; page 4: ©Leo de Wys, Inc.; pages 6, 7, and
21: ©Jeffrey Aaronson/Network Aspen; page 9: ©Jodi
Cobb/National Geographic Image Collection; page 10:
©John Isaac; page 13: ©Richard Lobell; pages 14–15:
©Guillermo Aldana Espinosa/National Geographic
Image Collection; page 17: ©Jason Lauré; page 18:
©Suzanne Murphy-Larronde/DDB Stock Photography;
page 22: ©Michael Philip Manheim/International Stock;
page 23: ©Esbin-Anderson/Photo Network.

**Library of Congress
Cataloging-in-Publication Data**
Markham, Lois.
Harvest/ by Lois Markham.
        p.   cm. —(World celebrations and ceremonies)
    Includes bibliographical references and index.
    Summary: Describes how people in various
countries around the world give thanks for the harvest.
    ISBN 1-56711-275-7 (lib. bdg. : alk. paper)
    1. Harvest festivals—Juvenile literature.
[1. Harvest festivals. 2. Festivals. 3. Holidays.]
I. Title. II. Series.
GT4502.M37   1999
394.26—dc21   98-15096
                                                                CIP
                                                                AC

⊙ CONTENTS ⊙

⑥ INTRODUCTION ⑥

Food! It's tasty and satisfying, and we need it to survive. That's why harvest—the gathering of crops—is a time for celebrating and for giving thanks. In many countries, foods are grown in summer and are harvested in late summer and early fall. But summer and fall occur at different times of the year in different places. In the northern part of the world, summer occurs in June through August. In the south, summer is December through February.

No matter when a harvest occurs, it is a joyful time. In Brazil, people welcome the grape harvest with a winemaking festival called *Festa da Uva* (FES-ta da OO-va). In London, England, fish and fruit sellers wear costumes for a harvest-time parade.

Harvest is a time to show appreciation as well as to have fun. In India, people celebrate the gathering of rice with a festival. They decorate their cows to thank them for their help in plowing the fields. In the United States, families and friends share a Thanksgiving feast. Harvest celebrations bring people closer together—people from the same community, and even from different parts of the world!

Brazil

Brazil is a nation of immigrants. They have come from other countries to live in Brazil. One of the country's biggest harvest festivals was started by Italian immigrants. They came from Italy after World War II ended in 1945.

Many of these immigrants settled along Brazil's southern coast. There, they found good conditions for growing grapes and making wine. This is a tradition in Italy and in other European countries. Now new Brazilians have a celebration for the grape harvest during the month of January. It is called *Festa da Uva* (FES-ta da OO-va), which means "Festival of the Grape" in Portuguese, the main language of Brazil.

In Jundiai, about 20 miles north of the city of São Paulo, *Festa da Uva* is truly an Italian-Brazilian event. People dress in traditional Italian costumes and taste the wines. A woman is crowned "Miss *Uva*," or "Miss Grape." People enjoy music and dancing, and they eat lots of fruit, pasta, and pizza.

This colorful mask looks as if it was made from a rich harvest of fruits.

In Brazil's southern state of Rio Grande do Sul, German immigrants celebrate their beer-making season with a festival. It is called *Sud Oktoberfest* (sud ok-TOH-bur-fest). Men dress in shorts with suspenders attached. They are called *lederhosen* (la-der-HO-sen). Women wear dresses with tight waistbands, called *dirndls* (DERN-duhls). People sing and dance, and they taste the beers they have made.

All over Brazil, and especially in the northern town of Campina Grande, people who worship in the Catholic faith celebrate the feast of Saint John. He was a holy man who lived during the time of the Bible. In Brazil, Catholics believe Saint John is responsible for the harvest of corn and of a local green bean. The feast of Saint John takes place in June. Campina Grande has one of the largest Saint John's parties in the world. Families decorate a park with balloons, lights, and ornaments.

Key for All Country Maps
★ *Capital city*   ■ *Major city*

Ⓜany parts of Brazil have warm weather and get lots of rain—perfect for growing many crops.

CHINA

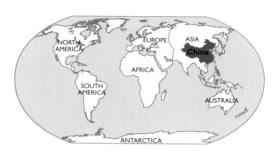

China's Mid-Autumn Festival honors the harvest, a full moon, and a woman called the Moon Maiden. The Chinese have a lunar calendar. It is based on the movement of the moon around Earth. The Mid-Autumn Festival is celebrated on the fifteenth day of the eighth month. At that time, there is always a full moon.

The festival is a national holiday in China. It is celebrated in big cities, such as Guangzhou, and in the countryside. On this day, families gather to share a festive meal. After the meal, everyone goes outdoors to look at the bright moon. They eat small round treats called "mooncakes." The mooncakes are often filled with a paste made from red beans or from the seeds of a lotus flower. Some mooncakes have a duck's egg in the middle.

The Mid-Autumn Festival is a time for families to gather together. This family lives in northeast China, where wheat is grown.

China produces more rice and wheat than almost any other country in the world.

The Mid-Autumn Festival is more than 2,000 years old. No one is quite sure how it got started. But at one time, it was probably a festival to give thanks for the rice harvest. Many Chinese also think of this holiday as a time to honor the Moon Maiden. They believe that she was the wife of a god. One day the Moon Maiden stole a magical drink from her husband, and she sipped it. The drink gave her the power to fly. She flew to the moon to escape her husband, who would be angry because she had stolen his magical drink.

A man sells bunches of the large radishes that are grown in China.

When families get together for the Mid-Autumn Festival, they tell the Moon Maiden's story. They also go on picnics and enjoy the out-doors in celebration of nature.

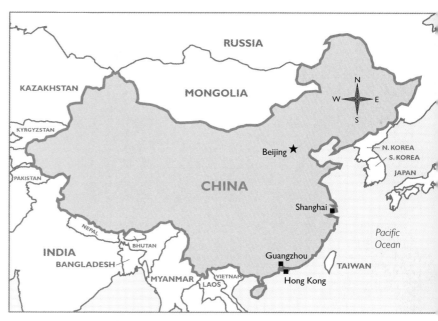

ENGLAND

People have been eating grains for thousands of years. Grain comes from special kinds of food plants. Oats, wheat, and rice are grains. Before there were machines to cut grain, harvest was very hard work. In England's many farming villages, everyone helped with the harvest. The end of all that hard work was celebrated with a festival called Harvest Home. It is still celebrated in some villages. People sing and dance. They also decorate the village and church with plants they have harvested.

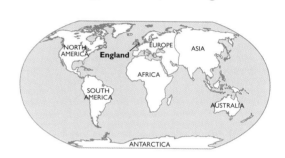

Long ago, the English believed that the spirit of their grain lived in the last sheaf, or bundle, that was cut. So the last sheaf was formed into the shape of a person. It was called a "corn dolly." (In England, *corn* is the general word for "grain.") The corn dolly kept the plant's spirit alive until the next planting in the spring. The dolly was even given a name. Families took it to church for a harvest service. Then they hung it in a barn until spring. Corn dollies are still made today.

Some places in England have traditions for marking the end of a harvest. In Stratford-upon-Avon, the work year ended after all the crops were gathered. Farm workers went to town to look for new jobs for the winter. They carried their tools to advertise their skills.

England's weather is mild for a country that is so far north. Wheat and oats are two of England's most important crops.

During harvest time, fruit and fish sellers parade in London wearing suits covered with pearl buttons.

Shopkeepers gave the workers a festival called the "Mop Fair."

In London, England's capital city, fish and fruit sellers parade in suits covered with pearl buttons. The parade takes place on a Sunday during harvest time. The couple with the best costumes are called the "Pearly King and Queen."

INDIA

Rice is an important crop in India. The rice harvest is celebrated in many ways around the country. In the southern state of Tamil Nadu, people celebrate the first rice harvest of the year and the end of the rainy season. The celebration takes place in January. It is a three-day festival known as *Pongal* (PONG-awl).

India has rich farmland in the valleys below the tall Himalaya Mountains. India is one of the world's biggest producers of rice.

On the first day of *Pongal*, people go to a temple and offer gifts to their gods to thank them for the rain that helps the rice grow. On the second day, women make a treat with rice, sugar, milk, nuts, and dried fruits. If the milk overflows the pot while the treat is cooking, the coming year is supposed to be a good one. As soon as the milk boils, the women shout, "*Pongal! Pongal!*" The word *pongal* means "boil" in the Tamil language, which is spoken in Tamil Nadu. On the third day of *Pongal*, cows are honored for their help with gathering the harvest.

A woman decorates her home in southern India, just as people do for the festival called Onam.

People paint their horns bright colors and decorate them with flowers.

In the southern state of Kerala, the ten-day harvest festival is called *Onam* (OH-nahm). It is celebrated in August and September. Children decorate their homes with colorful mats woven out of flowers. People visit temples to give thanks for the harvest. They feast on rice, vegetables, and sweet puddings. Boat races are held in ponds. There may be as many as 100 men rowing the boats.

In the northern state of Punjab, people celebrate harvest in April and May. The name of this festival is *Baisakhi* (Bah-SAH-kee). It is an important religious day for an Indian group called Sikhs. They begin the festival with a two-day reading from their holy book. Then everyone sits down together for a feast. After the meal, men dance the *bhangra* (bah-HANG-ra). It is a popular and lively dance about the cycles of the farming year.

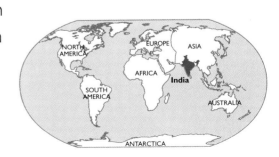

Israel

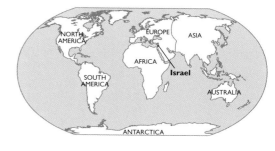

Imagine an eight-day picnic in the fall. That will give you some idea of the harvest holiday of *Sukkot* (soo-KOHT). It is celebrated by Jewish people all over the world, but especially in Israel.

For this celebration, families make a simple building called a *sukkah* (soo-KAH). They use tree branches for the roof. When they are in the *sukkah*, they can see the sky between the branches. Children hang fruit from the roof. The *sukkah* is always outdoors, even in the crowded capital city of Jerusalem. The *sukkah* may be on a porch or in the backyard.

This simple building honors the Jews who lived in the desert thousands of years ago. *Sukkahs* are also reminders of the huts that farmers lived in during the harvest. They stayed in huts to be near their crops. For the eight days of *Sukkot*, a family eats its meals in the *sukkah*. Some families even sleep there.

Another harvest festival is *Shavuoth* (sha-vu-OHT). The word *Shavuoth* means the "Festival of Weeks" in Hebrew, Israel's main language. This festival is held in the spring. It takes place at the end of the barley harvest and the beginning of the wheat harvest. People celebrate by eating *blintzes* (BLINT-sez), thin pancakes filled with cheese and sometimes fruit. They also decorate their homes and synagogues with flowers. A synagogue is a Jewish place of worship. During *Shavuoth*, Jews go to synagogue to give thanks to God for the harvest. They also give thanks for the *Torah* (toe-RAH), the laws that God gave them to live by.

A man in a sukkah *holds four symbols of a good harvest. They are a lemon-like fruit called a "citron," twigs from a willow tree and from a myrtle bush, and long leaves from a palm tree.*

Israel is a small country on the Mediterranean Sea. Its most important crops are citrus fruits, such as oranges and lemons.

MEXICO

The Huichol people live in the Sierra Madre Mountains, in north-west Mexico. They have lived there for almost 500 years. Today, they still keep their old customs alive, such as their harvest celebrations.

The Huichol begin their harvest ceremonies early in October. The most important one is the Ceremony of the Squashes. It is done to protect children and to teach them about their people. During the ceremony, young Huichol learn about the trail their parents follow to the desert. That is where they gather peyote, a small catcus plant that is very important in the Huichol's religion.

The Ceremony of the Squashes takes place in the center of a village. The adults face east while chanting. (*Chanting* means saying or singing something over and over again.) The chant describes how the squashes visit the Huichol's gods. While the adults chant, young children shake rattles. The children wear two crossed sticks on their heads. The sticks have colorful yarn woven into diamond shapes. These shapes are nicknamed "god's eyes." They are symbols of the four directions of the compass—north, south, east, and west. Each diamond represents a journey.

Mexico's weather is very warm near the coast and cooler in the mountains. The country's most important crops are coffee, corn, and wheat.

UNITED STATES

Monterrey

MEXICO

*Pacific
Ocean*

Guadalajara

Mexico
City ★

*Gulf of
Mexico*

BELIZE

GUATEMALA

N
W — E
S

A family takes part in the Ceremony of the Squashes. On the left are colorful "god's eyes" made from sticks and yarn.

Near the village center is a post with a hanging piece of cloth called a "sash." Squashes that have just been harvested are placed at the bottom of the post. There is one squash for each child in the ceremony. The sash is a symbol of the path that the squashes travel.

NIGERIA

There are many groups of people in Nigeria. Each one has its own holidays and celebrations. Singing, dancing, and costume parties are part of many Nigerian harvest celebrations.

Southeast of the city of Lagos, the Igbo celebrate the New Yam Festival. It marks the beginning of harvest time, and is held in July or August. People offer gifts of cows, nuts, wines, and yams to the Earth Goddess. It is their way of showing thanks for their yams and other crops.

Nigeria has warm weather all year. Two of its most important crops are peanuts and cassava plants. Cassavas are used to make a kind of flour.

On the first day of the celebration, a family roasts and eats many birds. One roasted bird is saved for the second day. On that day, the family gathers at the house of the oldest member. Everyone eats the roasted bird. It is passed around in a ceremony called "the handing around of the bird."

Another harvest celebration is the Argungun Fishing Festival. It is held in February and March in northern Nigeria. The festival marks the end of the growing season and the harvest. Nearly 5,000 men gather in the Argungun River for a contest. They use nets or hollowed-out vegetables called

Dancing is always a central part of Nigerian harvest festivals.

"gourds" to try and catch the largest fish. A prize is given to the winner.

The southern city of Benin holds the festival of *Irovbode* (ee-ROHV-boh-day) at the end of the rainy season and the harvest. During the festival, men and women are introduced to each other. They hope to meet their future marriage partners.

17

PUERTO RICO

The Caribbean island of Puerto Rico has many mountains. Few areas are good for growing crops. But one plant that does grow well in the mountains is the coffee tree. Coffee is grown and harvested by hand. It is hard work. When the coffee harvest ends in February or March, Puerto Rico's coffee farmers are ready to celebrate.

In the town of Maricao, southwest of the capital city of San Juan, there is a Coffee Harvest Festival. Families enjoy watching a parade of colorful floats. A float is a moving platform that is decorated for a parade. At the Coffee Harvest Festival, the floats are covered with coffee trees, banana trees, and flowers. Many girls who come to the festival wear long, wide skirts.

These girls are enjoying the Coffee Harvest Festival in the town of Maricao.

Boys dress in cowboy outfits. People listen to the happy tunes of Puerto Rican music and taste local foods. Dishes include rice with peas, fried bananas, and pastries filled

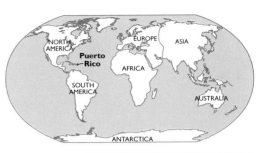

with fruit. Many desserts and beverages are made with coffee beans, including ice cream, pudding, and cake.

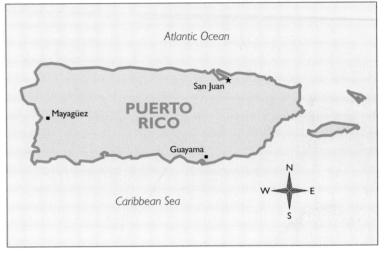

In the 1500s, people from Spain settled in Puerto Rico. They started farming sugar cane, the plant that sugar comes from. There are still some sugar cane growers in Puerto Rico today. In April, the town of San German holds a festival at the end of the sugar harvest. People celebrate with music, crafts, and food. They also have exhibits about sugar cane plants.

Another crop grown in Puerto Rico is a fruit called a "plantain." Plantains look like bananas. In October, the northern town of Corozal holds the National Plantain Festival. At the festival, there are exhibits about local crafts and farming.

Puerto Rico is an island in the Caribbean Sea. The country's many mountains are good places for growing coffee trees.

RUSSIA

When you look at a map of the world, you will notice that one country is bigger than any

Russia is the biggest country in the world. Most of its farmland is in the western part of the country, where a lot of wheat is grown.

other. Russia spreads across the continents of Europe and Asia. Much of the country is farmland. For hundreds of years, Russian farmers have celebrated the harvest.

In a traditional Russian harvest, the first and last sheaves of wheat are very important. People once believed that the seeds from these sheaves had special power. Some families still decorate these sheaves with flowers or ribbons. The sheaves are taken to church to be blessed by a priest. Then they are brought into a farmer's house and placed in a special corner or under a religious picture.

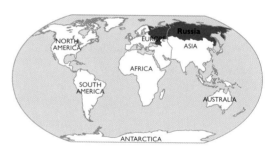

Later the sheaves are mixed with the seeds that will be used to plant next year's crop. Some farmers believe this will bring a good harvest.

Another traditional harvest ceremony is the Curling of the Beard. A patch of grain, called the "beard," is left uncut in the field. People decorate the patch with ribbons and bend the heads of the grain to the ground. Some Russians believe that the spirit of the harvest hides in this patch of uncut grain. The

Some Russian children dress in traditional clothing for special occasions, such as harvest ceremonies.

Curling of the Beard gives the power of the grain back to the earth to provide a healthy field for the next growing season.

UNITED STATES

The United States is one of the few countries in the world with a national harvest holiday. This holiday is called Thanksgiving. It started with the English settlers called Pilgrims, who landed in Massachusetts in November 1620. During their first winter, there was little to eat and many people died. The next spring, Native Americans showed the Pilgrims how to plant corn and other vegetables.

A family shares a Thanksgiving feast.

⊚ · ⊚ · ⊚ · ⊚ · ⊚ · ⊚ · ⊚ · ⊚ · ⊚ · ⊚

The United States has a lot of farmland in the Midwest, near the center of the country. Wheat and corn are important crops.

⊚ · ⊚ · ⊚ · ⊚ · ⊚ · ⊚ · ⊚ · ⊚ · ⊚ · ⊚

The Pilgrims grew many crops. They wanted to thank God and also the Native Americans for the good harvest. So they had a harvest festival.

Few facts are known about this first Thanksgiving. It may have taken place in October. We do know that fish, ducks, and geese were roasted over a fire. The Native Americans brought deer meat, which is called "venison." Squashes and cranberries may have been eaten, too.

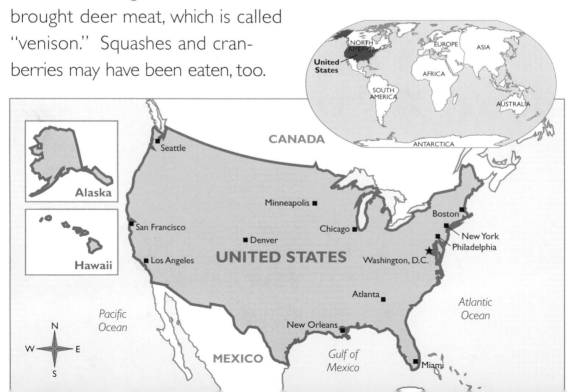

For three days, the Pilgrims and Native Americans ate, gave thanks, and played games. Thanksgiving was not made a national holiday until 1863. In 1941, the fourth Thursday of November became the official day of celebration.

Thanksgiving is not the only harvest festival celebrated in the United States. Many Native Americans have harvest celebrations that are much older than the Thanksgiving holiday. The Hopi people dance the Corn Dance to give thanks for the harvest. The Miwok of California have an acorn harvest celebration. One of the country's newest holidays is *Kwanzaa*

An African-American family celebrates Kwanzaa.

(KWAHN-zuh). It is celebrated by African Americans during the last week of December. Though it is a winter holiday, it is based on African harvest festivals.

Glossary

chant To say or sing something over and over again.

corn dolly A human figure made out of stalks of grain.

float A moving platform that is decorated for a parade.

grain Seeds of a kind of food plant, such as oats, wheat, and rice.

harvest The gathering of crops.

immigrant Someone from another nation who comes to a country to live there.

lunar calendar A calendar based on the movement of the moon around Earth.

sheaf Several grain stalks gathered together in a bundle.

synagogue A Jewish place of worship

yam A root vegetable that tastes like a sweet potato.

Further Reading

Corwin, Judith Hoffman. *Harvest Festivals Around the World*. Morristown, NJ: Julian Messner, 1995.

Hoyt-Goldsmith, Diane. *Celebrating Kwanzaa*. New York: Holiday House, 1993.

Kalman, Bobbie. *We Celebrate the Harvest* (Holidays & Festivals series). New York: Crabtree Publishing, 1986.

Miller, Marilyn F. *Thanksgiving* (World of Holidays series). Chatham, NJ: Raintree/Steck-Vaughn, 1998.

Rosen, Mike. *Autumn Festivals*. The Bookwright Press, 1990.

Whitlock, Ralph. *Thanksgiving and Harvest*. Vero Beach, FL: Rourke Enterprises, 1987.

Tourism Web Sites

Brazil: http://www.brazilinfo.com

China: http://www.Chinatourpage.com

England: http://www.visitbritain.com

India: http://www.tourindia.com

Israel: http://www.goisrael.com

Mexico: http://www.mexico-travel.com

Nigeria: http://www.sas.upenn.edu/African_Studies/Country_Specific/Nigeria.htm

Puerto Rico: http://www.Welcome.toPuertoRico.org

Russia: http://www.tours.ru

United States: http://www.united-states.com

Index